WATER IS THE FIRST WORLD

WATER IS THE FIRST WORLD

SUSAN ANDREWS GRACE

COTEAU BOOKS

Edited by Anne Szumigalski.

Cover photograph by Courtney Milne (Photo-Synthesis Inc.) taken from Oahu, Hawaii.

Author photograph by Honor Kever.

Book design by Shelley Sopher, Coteau Books.

Typeset by Val Jakubowski, Coteau Books.

Printed and bound in Canada.

The publisher gratefully acknowledges the financial assistance of the Saskatchewan Arts Board, the Canada Council and the Department of Communications.

Canadian Cataloguing in Publication Data

Grace, Susan Andrews, 1949-
Water is the first world
Poems.
ISBN 1-55050-018-X
I. Title.
PS8563.R234W3 1991 C811/.54 C91-097024-6
PR9199.3.G723W3 1991

Coteau Books
401 - 2206 Dewdney Avenue
Regina, Saskatchewan
S4R 1H3

for the mothers

& especially Mary Elizabeth Grace
who first brought me to the water

CONTENTS

it's possible to fly, really

she was able to see, quite clearly
as she glided along a little above the grass
how important it is to get above it all
to not notice the voluptuous older woman
on the couch, her corseted breasts pointed skyward
not wonder who she was and why she was there
thighs girdled and stockinged in flesh tones
but instead to wake the children straight away
pack their frozen lunches, get them to school on time

then to think back to the early-bird swim that morning
and how she felt coming home
on top of things
not bothered by time and gravity   she walked
the city sidewalk to her yard where suddenly
they all were suspended   gravity and time
and she was gliding in the air so surely

the door opened

and wind rushed in filling spaces
with songs and singing. down
the long hall she went kicking
at a ball, graceful arcs of her
skipping legs, arms swinging to this side
and that, as she leapt to the singing.
all the men who gathered round wanted to follow
and take pictures but could not. she was no longer
touching ground or ball.

It wasn't on his own

that Jerry flew. It was through his poems
which drew him over the white land
fuzzed by sepia bushes here and there,
leaving the porch with the one wooden
chair, to be carried along by words
through the air. And when it was time
to come down he pulled on the cord
which silvered him slowly to the snow.

one hell of a wind

don't you know, he said to himself,
coming up from the cellar
to see his wife standing coolly and strangely
translucent, in what used to be his house
now blown to smithereens.

(the tornado had torn through his land
and sent his wife into the wind
while he was down cellar for some hootch and a rollie)

people all around said they saw her
flying crazily through the sky
later found her body in a creek bed some miles away

and he had missed it all, the one chance
to see his wife in the sky

floating

she needed to get above it all
the guide from the forest told her
he was able to take off his head
put it in the crook of a fir tree
and watch himself from there   she too
could try it

find a way to keep her head upstairs
her body doing things downstairs
above it all the way   at the same time
not wasting a moment

the guide came to help but was unable
to find her   she was scattered so

her hands were in the kitchen while her
heart was with the children at school   her stomach
was in the dining room dreaming meals made
by her mother while her breasts, sucked dry, were tucked
beneath the pillow in her bedroom awaiting her husband
her mind was absorbed in a book about a man
who paints all the people purples and greens
her feet were in the garden gathering strength

the guide gave up & went back to the glade
in the forest to call her name

crock

the titter of china as the cupboard door
is opened palters the secret life
of dishes shut away in the dark, a sensuous
cave of cups upon saucers, tumultuous touch
of bowls to jugs, plates missionaried by other
plates, glasses slipping inside glasses
my heart falls to pieces as I open the cupboard

Bottom Line

There's a pink line in the sky, you've probably seen it
just above the horizon and over the hills
where all the women go.

All the women who climb out of the black bucket
flattened thin as wafers, to slip into a place
on the other side of this world
where fruits grow and so does justice;
ready-made salads and cut flowers for everyone.

Donna, who left her husband and sons
(just overnight, mind you)
to go through that line in the sky
found she never had to weed a garden.
Only plant it, the way she liked, barefoot on a full moon
using her big toe to make trenches
for lacy carrot seed, plump soaked peas,
microscopic lettuce and marigold airplanes
and flat zinnias and weird borage.
There vegetables grow direct from seed to salad
flowers from seed to bouquet.

A Practical Vision

He stands at the foot of her bed. She's eighteen. She wonders: is this the man I am to marry, should I watch for this face throughout my life? She marries someone who doesn't look like him and wonders if this is a mistake. Every once in a while she wonders: "Who was it so beautiful at the foot of my bed?" But mostly she doesn't think about him, gets on with her life until one day she discovers him at her side, his arm around her shoulder. She is walking across the steel bridge, wondering "Do people see him?" A biker whizzes by, right through where he is. He is unhurt, smiles and winks at her. When she gets to work he leaves her but he's there again when she comes down the stairs from the dusty office. He walks her home.

He doesn't talk out loud to her because he doesn't need to. Angels are like that. He hears her thoughts to him and talks back in the most astonishingly natural way.

She's had her share of fantasies in adult life. Mostly about a boyfriend who would take her to movies, put his arm around her shoulder, kiss her on the cheek. In this relationship she would be allowed all imperfections and it wouldn't matter. The boyfriend would see her whole self and like her anyway. She just hadn't expected this angel.

He begins to come downtown to the office, when she needs him or sometimes he's there at home, in the laundry room, just company, as she sorts the laundry and loads the washer with all the dirty things. The day the basement floods, he's there comforting her. Of course he doesn't do any of the physical work, so he's not in the way.

She finally decides that it doesn't matter that he's an angel, he'll do

pre-knowledge

red hair cut short
a Byronic love lock trailing
the nape of her neck
cape flowing in the wind
she is a modern Wicca eating ice cream
her muscled dancer legs
squeezing the white stallion

she is transparent
the stallion's eyes blink modestly as he
lifts his front legs   she stands on one hand
and he lifts his back legs
she licks her ice cream once more
as they ascend
the stallion leisurely loping the sky

Burning the Apple Tree

I hit you hard on your barrel chest
and the nightmare begins
breathe   one thousand and one
one thousand and two
your chest rises and falls
dead air escapes you
we share my breath here
in the living room's pink light
until the ambulance and your ashen son
carry you away

you're the man across the street
who never smiles
and scowls at the children
if they get too near your lawn
already ruined by roots

later I feel you near me when I am
furiously burning pieces
of tree roots in my back yard
shivering and gagging on the memory
of the phlegm which foamed
into my mouth when I breathed
into you and you moaned
a dead rattle

I feel you near me,
the cool draft of air, your presence
near my face and I can't tell if you
have forgiven me or if you
are blaming me for the indignity
you suffered on your living room floor.

In his paintings

people float in an unearthly manner
but he barely notices. He only paints
surrounded by love, complete and unjealous
of the small woman who sits beside him.
In the picture, her hand floats over
his hand emerging from the grey sweater.

He lives in France, was awakened in Russia.
Born Jewish, he lives like a Christian,
loves his wife so purely she appears
once a year, hovering

water is the first world

the whole world
here I return to the boiler room
of my mother's irish heart, waves
rush and slap, fingers fingering pruney skin

my name is called from the pale green
purl just now opening

I surge
into the ear's labyrinth, swim
its canals, attentive to a beat,
flesh-hammer, marking the way

swimmer's ear

it comes from using the water for a pillow
rhythmically turning for air to listen
to the sound under *slap and slosh and slam*
the sound over *tingle and gurgle and tick*
now it is always with me   the sound
when I turn my head, move my jaw

it comes from using the water for a pillow
water conducts better than feathers
I choose the cold splash in early morning
rather than the man under the blue quilt
his heart pulsing through the down

I hear the beginning, particles rushing
home to their mothers, water
lost in the bones of my ear

laps

here I am again to untie the knot in my shoulder, to soothe
the sinew and listen for solutions in the slap
and shock of water swallows in my breath

here I find the right words
to quilt a drunkard's path and embroider convolvulus vines
on the white tablecloth and a sigh
that walks with me to and from the water

walks and sighs are transitions to the vertical world

to swim is to put thoughts in their rightful place, to stuff
ideas with sound and cotton
until it tangles
and again it's time to untie the knot in my shoulder

to swim

in water are first sounds

and I hear them there
as it separates and with fingers, hand, arm
I enable it to fly up and yield
to the silver air so eager to swallow it

just fine

I see him beside me in the next lane
also yawning in his crawl
a sleepy roll closer to my side
we swim a few more lengths and
I know by his strokes he is with me
I imagine caressing his bald head
feel his hairy arms ripple around me
I am languid in those furry long legs

at breakfast when you ask
HOW WAS YOUR SWIM?
I say, FINE JUST FINE,
the goggle man
asleep in my ear

what is to come

gravity has no business here

a raven I see with my eyes closed
comes to the swim, follows me,
whispers he knows, he knows
my death and its time.
The place he will not tell.
His wing tip blends with the right arc of my goggle
as he says hurry, hurry past the tiles
at the bottom of the pool

Here I trust black-winged whispers.
Safe in motherwater, there's promise:
blue-green sunlight dappling
my place of no measure.

illumination

swimming along beside me they
whisper their names:
freshet and rill, spring tide, ebb tide and flow, furrow and
swell, headwaters, surf and spume, bloodstream.

O

Do you love me now as you did
when your love was round as the O
of blood oranges from the market in Via Montebello?

for years we quickened memory
recalling the name of the back street
our building let on to   now it is lost
as the O that was a mouth to lick and push
a tongue into Saturday mornings in bed

that O of spring blowing out Easter candles
alabaster inside an egg's shell

Thought Disturbance

I do some of my best thinking
on my back. I've told you that
but you continually misunderstand
and leap
to express unflagging love.
You clutter my thinking
so I lie on my side and this too
you find irresistable. Sitting and walking's
the same. We leave behind us
a trail of my thinking— pleasured.

Leaning Tower

The wooden stairs were 400 years old, they
creaked and there was no railing, only you
to guide me.
Coming down was hard.

I thought I was
afraid of heights.

I think
I was afraid of you.

In your air

My words are suspended, in your air,
dried up before you hear them.
I want you to come down to the water
feel the warm currents on top,
the colder ones around our ankles
I will stretch out in the water
the spool bones of my spine as even
as a string of pearls
free of the logical weight of air.
Everything I say to you will be clear,
will swim behind your eyes
smoothly as deepwater fish.

Church of Santa Susanna

We sit in filtered four o'clock sun
listening to interminable Pange Lingua sung
by celibates behind the altar

you not understanding any more than I
what I try to tell you or Susanna's
story, one I can't quite remember
except she was a virgin, pure, and something
about bathing. By this time,
I am crying.

We merge into the dusk and jostle of exiles
rushing to apartments and rooms. Prayer
hide behind my tongue.

Because of you I have forsaken prayer, light,
new doorways— each a different rapture.
In this church only virgins are allowed ecstasy.

You move hesitantly, hands deep in green pockets
fingering bread and tobacco crumbs— wondering, I suppose,
what is expected of a protestant boy in Rome.

Pasquita

we celebrated little easter
in the purple hills, a jar of water
planted in the ground
we cooked eggs over an open fire
ate them with olives and
came home on the bus full of sun

later, seeing the full moon in the electric sky
we were jolted along in the lurching bus
and a man told us it's time for bambinos

our cave of love reddened its walls

bronchitis

the first breath of outside air each morning begins again
the fits of coughing, spasms
pushing out my ribs barrelling
my chest, its staves are swords encircling the air locked
below tiny obstructions, daisy chains, turning
my voice huskier every day

the air, you see, is not allowed me, I must
take only a little because if I do not stop
myself I might take a lot, forget and enjoy
this love you are offering
and then I know you

off you would run to the train station saying no, no
you can't have it any more holding it up above
your head out of my reach dancing before me running
away and would hop the express to Malaga, watch
bullfights all day and all night
so I stay the way I am, coughing

to Spain

the train nudges hills, falling sun
a yellow flan behind the dark
turtle tree
                    I breathe quietly
beside you
all the way to Barcelona (saffron
soup) Madrid (baby shirts)
Torremolinos (a blind bull)

your hands

don't come near me when you've loved someone else
I'm not ready

don't come near me
when I've just thought about betrayal,
her blonde roundness still fresh in my mind
your hands all over her

I sat

I sat still while you lusted
for attention and perfumed women,
a particular silly woman who liked
your shirt
I sat at home, confused
at work, tired,
vaguely aware

O MONOGAMOUS ME, A WALKING SONG, TO AID IN MEDITATION ON AND INTEGRATION OF DIVERGING OPINION ABOUT THE MEANING OF COMMITMENT

O monogamous me, I could not rise
above my upbringing.
Great loves lurked at every turn
and still I stayed for you, for you.

No lavender lake with swans

just you and you
and the absence of you.

Yes means I will be yours, you'll be
what you want with a woman who
slips onto you
like a sweater on a hook
while I'm out.

midnight gardener

you are the subject of my poems   you
bursting at the seams with energy
for trimming & pulling & burning fires
until dawn   fires
of branches and poplar leaves
burning   who promise the moon
but can't get home on time for supper
burning   who keeps putting off reading
until he finds the book on procrastination
burning   who lights my herb garden on fire
letting only parsley survive
burning   who looks at his desk only to see
if a poem about him, the midnight gardener,
has been written yet

mice

to reassure me
you say they are just birds
without wings   I wonder
what is more horrible

a whole extended family's damage
deposit for a year's residence
the speckled house: turds
in the kitchen sink, cupboards,
pots, drawers, pans—
bubonic plague, regular plague,
septicemic plague, sylvatic plague,
deer fly fever, dandy fever, and
dreaded mouse fever

:or most horrible—
the fat family member   bird
I suppose   I saw scurry around my desk
last fall

in bed

I need to become part of the adult world again. you say you know the best way to relax me. oh no, not that I say, celibacy is the coming thing, did you know? you inch your way over until I say I need space too. Later, over there, you say that I know where it is in case I want it.
yes.

It is not the same

It is not the same for a man who suffers the passion of loving a God, crucified. He has great things to contemplate; his is a serious life. For a godless woman in love there are the small things to marvel at: gravity, green steps to the bath, the white towel, a child's silver cup.

one for each

these rings once were
one
    weight
and they anchored you with faith

until the sores began weeping
beneath the gold
oozing you free of me
and the ring

I took it to a goldsmith
who sliced it into three

a ring for each of the children I say
and I wear them all at once

libido

four a.m. I give the baby a drink of water stumble back into the
bedroom grope in the dark for the bed you say   stop don't get
back into bed close the door and lift that T-shirt I climb in anyway
say I'm too tired I worked late last night after you went to sleep
you say listen to the silence not a bird breath or child noise just the
sun hitting the roof peeking through the trees around the blinds
and you're pining for my body speaking of which we haven't
called the memorial society to order our funerals damn I say I
forgot and neither of us notice we've changed the subject

Selma Lagerlöf speaking
(1858 - 1940)

Cook it was who took us children there
to the Carolinian Medical Institute
said it was much finer than
the Royal Palace or the National Museum
but the watchman's wife who had the keys
did not want to let us see
the wondrous things
they argued and made us sit
eat cakes and drink coffee
imagine two cups each

It was the dressmaker's niece
who finally convinced the watchman's wife
that we should see at least
the finely coloured plaster casts
of limbs like fins
bodies born wrong
cancer and smallpox-ravaged parts

Cook said, Don't you think children
that this is quite marvellous
the watchman's wife agreed and she said
that was so because it was all real
and on we went to the big jars
that held a baby with two heads
a pair of club feet and hands with buds
where fingers might be

the second last thing we saw
was in the attic a closet like mine
but when the door opened
there was a neat row of skeletons
hanging like my clothes with the biggest one
taller than Mama's dresses
the skeleton of Long Lapska
a freak in her time said the watchman's wife

then Cook said, Oh to be a man
so that I could be a doctor
and come and go here all day long

the last thing Cook showed us
was in the basement
at the door the watchman's wife
said, No they're too young. Yes I thought
I shall never be as old as Cook
to like all of this

but she was tireless we entered the stench anyway
saw the bodies
all in a moment's look   saw them
those who had taken their lives
four in the tank crosswise
as if in a big double bed   a sad lot
but especially the young woman
dressed in a black threadbare coat

at home I stared hard at the painting of King Axel
our King Axel of Sweden on his deathbed
and asked him to please
take those bed covers from the picture
and go to the four people
to cover them in the watery bed
they looked so cold

and he knowing the ways of the dead
being a dead one himself
spread a light over them

Katherine Mansfield speaking
(1883 - 1923)

and some things I didn't want are here too, my Jack

here I find women are of a different order—
they teach me more than books.

health and a house,
sea and a garden,
are all I've ever wanted.

I dance through pain & coughing,
love for seven minutes, for
a whole life.

Mary E. Wilkins Freeman speaking
(1852 - 1930)

at first I did not like people
my women were strong as Sarah Penn
like Mother who revolted, moved
the entire family to the palatial barn
leaving the cramped house empty
(a statement to father who was off to buy horses)
joy and anger and resourcefulness were there
all of it   in those women

my stories were good

then Freeman came
the horseman flirt and drunk that he was
captured me   filled my heart
at fifty I married him   and two years later
he was in a sanitorium
drying out dead

after that my women were proud
and cautious like hefty Eliza Sam
who locked an unwanted suitor in a church overnight
so he might cool his ardour
asked the man she really loved to let him out at dawn
and then set to waiting twenty years to be wed

Charlotte Perkins Gilman speaking
(1860 - 1935)

i

up at four I punch a hole into the washwater
with my elbow   my room has the New England chill
iron until six   it is a regular day
see all my students   light supper
and to bed by ten   the moon outside
is full and bright as the body and mind
I am shaping to do the work

ii

big tears fall down my cheeks
onto my breast and the feeding Katharine
nothing more bitter than this
that even motherhood brings no joy
the yellow wallpaper is all around me now
and behind is the woman, clawing

the black cloud of marriage remains

Sylvia Ashton-Warner speaking
(b. 1908)

I should never have married him—
my work was more important, he said.

I was a forgotten girl teaching Maori
except for him
I could not have made words real
for the infants at school,
made travel a canoe, men
their uncles, music their favourite songs.
He was the key for me
to make keys for them.

It may not be apparent, but you and our babies
are everything to me, I told him
(he was boiling water for tea)
if I had to choose between the work and you
I would give it all up.

Still he said he would do more,
the housework, all the milking.

We drank our tea, ran off the dishes
and went to bed.

Evelyn Scott speaking
(1893 - 1963)

I've spent months huge and helpless
and hours trying to paint the red
baby carriage white   I imagine
I'll remain like this
the rest of my life (pregnant
and encouraging other writers)

Doctor Januario took off my clothes,
his cold eyes and emerald watch fob,
his immaculate clothing
felt me all over
said that I am healthy   the baby is in
the correct position
I can have the child
without any trouble

I wish
I could have my baby alone

Adrienne Rich (b. 1921)
speaking in my head

. . . only death will free us from one another

I chased my daughter down the street
scratching half-moons on her upper arm—
I brought her home,
my jaw sore from clenching

the pumping was my own heart returning
blood, also hers fresh under my fingernails

when the fire of our wills had faded
she fell asleep in my arms

at the beginning

the river frozen and shifting
wrapped in white, blood
cursing my ears, I shiver
know the verdict

only eight weeks
and easy to dispose of you

the river flows on, invites me
to return to where you began

I stand and the white sheet falls
naked, I tell you yes

in the garden patch

the green cabbage squats
on moist black loam
veining goodness

over this northern soil
poised as if to birth you
I am weeding and wondering
who will you be

one kick if you're Molly
two if you're Patrick

motherdeaf you sleep
on this Saskatchewan soil
these Irish names

a whale complex

I encapsule you   symbiotic one in
my belly

I the whale lady
swim from runny noses to boiling pots
in anger and hunger

you sap me   taking cells
to fatten your flesh

out out out with you now
no   don't you dare
I'm in charge here

swimming

hot blue scent rises
on the white alfalfa path
as I carry you down
into the purple slough

we join   stretch out
to lie in the water
you squirm in the hull
scare prairie minnows   fluttering

until quieted
a muscle hammock to sway and soothe you
sleep   play with your toes   sleep
sweet alfalfa
sleep

overdue

late, late, you're going to be late
the stars are falling, falling
shining through your eyelids,
patting on your eardrums,
crystals are forming, amniotic ice
there's danger, danger, the pink of summer
is gone, bumbling in the light
it's time, time to come out, you're late
stars shoot and the earth quakes,
my corduroy tunnel pulls, is pulling,
you are late, you are late, you are late

early labour day

I tread carefully today on swollen ankles
loose ligaments wobbling
my pelvic carriage rocks
gently your bone lodge, your
ominous calm
you quiver, suck your thumb
for comfort

then cry out loud, walls are collapsing, vortices pull—
you push out the red plug, drain
the amniotic sea
it is begun

your father hears your call   gets ready
rows out to meet you

my child

he's there, the doctor with red hair
apologizes but not for the tethering, stirrups, instruments
it's for his loss of control
he's sorry

dream ocean moonlight
she's squatting mare screams flails
rope floating between hind legs

they've brought in a machine
they say there are only thirty minutes left
for what I want to ask the green faces
they do not understand the sea

five men on the beach dry
cold white colt-tugging

now they have something to do
they don't see the wave
I am safe in its trough if they will
just leave me

husband, ashen-faced, this is all his fault,
he worries
there's a bubble in the IV tubing
blood chases it up the plastic rope
the tugging the tugging
mare's eyes reel in terror

thud, cat's on the instrument table, great! now their sterile
field is contaminated, somebody take that cat home

no

it's not the cat, only a clumsy nurse, she's reassuring,
says at least the baby will have a
beautiful face   turns away,
no fetal tone, she says, another green face says
27 minutes

do something

I hear myself moan
o god and
my mother

do something

screams
yours
mine
hair black slippery
hands of your father
the mare   moonlight
pulling   pulling
blood of you
blood of me
my child

Loom

The baby is on my knee. I am wearing a navy sweater and there are white flannelette nubs on it and milky spit in my hair. I remember a baby's mind doesn't grow in layers like an onion or an artichoke, instead it's woven in a complex pattern of under and over: fabric of experience and memory and together we are watching it. Language here today, gone tomorrow, reappears next month after mastery of stair climbing, dish towel snatching, key hiding. We stare at the back yard outside the kitchen window blinded by sun and brilliant snow, both of us exhausted.

making milk

I feign play with chicken bones
at supper times, covertly
grind them into meal
for you, to suck, tugging at my teeth,
sapping my spine, making porous my pelvis,
to grow hard baby long bones
weave nests of fat cells, knit dimples
for arms and legs

mineral strong, an umbilical white rope
connects us, my last chance
to grow beyond my body

Chrism

You are shriven now of our sin, the water
on your head does not
make you cry, salt
on your tongue
makes you taste
and you're awake
to feel the chrism
on your face. I see

the subtle bodies compress to fit you
who wears my father's white gown
and my husband's ring. I,

in catholic dark and donegal tweed,
feel my belly shrink
the more for loving your father
who is intent on his protestant hands
and their worry hives,
while his soul expands
to fill his body caught
in the blue woollen suit.

Misfire

i

You were down the hall, wired
by electrodes, your sleep
drawing alpha lines. I waited
hand over heart
mea culpa, your lip bled.

Then you sucked extension cords as if to
right the sin planted in your brain, not
petit mal or grand mal, just a small wrong, small.

ii

We sway, you clamped over my heart,
which stopped to watch you twitch
and stiff an eternity
until you squeezed out tears
penance on your cheeks and it's over.
Your lip bleeds again, swollen and big.
Big my baby and blue as the bonnet on your sweaty bald head.

iii

It is Paula who lives in the corner
by the bookcase, tells me the stem of
your brain was pinched by doctorfingers that
twisted your head so you could be born
face down easy for me.

I hang you upside down
to release the stem, demons,
from your tweeze of tiny vertebrae.

Gravity she says is all.

Gently you swing back and forth;
pleased you sing, giggle, sigh.

for Patrick

we are standing in the snow, you and I
we have stopped skiing because our noses are runny
it's your first time but you ski with grace
and skill beyond your four years

as I pull out your great grandmother's handkerchief
from my vest pocket, its edging not unlike the lace
of umber and mauve all around us in the snow
you become a ghost   a person
I do not know but have been with forever

                                        a dim fire
lit in Sweden (as I bend to wipe
your nose with white linen)
magically warms us

and when you are an acrobat

you will make somersaults
over and over
with your chin tucked under,
like this

green and bad

it's nearly fall   we are in the verandah
I am on the Toronto couch with a headache   you
fill the hole of an inner tube
there are green energies in the room
they come from the green door   you say
microscopic spots   like that   holding
pudgy thumb against forefinger
green energies from
all the people who pass through the doorway
you say that my headache is from the bad
energies   not like the green greens
but the ones that come down my hair
into my nose   up to bang on my headbone, to
bounce off my eyeballs
and when I ask how you know all that
you shrug

pre-med

again you want to see the diseases book
see the picture of the boy who got lice
and didn't let his mom comb out the nits
and scratched and scratched the itch
until it bled and his head puffed out
at the side and the bugs laid more eggs
until his head was all white and horrible
his neck sore like with the leprosy Ben
Hur's mother and sister had
and they had to live in a cave
so no one would catch it

I find the page
and when you've had your fill
you lie back on the floor
feeling your head over and over
the delicious horror

dead

you want to know about dead
and why the man across the street
goes by slowly in a black ambulance
no lights, no sirens
and is it the same as when the butterfly
died and you buried it, placed
a wooden grave marker over top
pencilled DEAD BUTTERFLY

it must be saturday morning

you're lifting the lid of my eye
to tell me it's time
for breakfast   and I'm thinking

look I gave you a place to grow
and milk from my body
I wash your clothes   love you
feel guilty   what more
can you want?

but before I can say any of this
you've pried open the other lid
and I see your concerned face
you repeat it's time for breakfast
and ask if it is called november
because it knows

why I'm not there at night

you want to know if the needle
that's stuck into my arm hurts me
and why the medicine has to go
into my blood so fast
and if it's having a race
with the pneumonia
what will it be like
if the medicine loses
and why I'm not there at night
to make supper
and why I left you asleep
on the bed we shared
to go to the hospital
and why Christopher's mommy was there
when you woke up
and then you say you don't care
any more   you kiss me hard
and say I like Christopher's mommy better
anyway

work day

you're going to your job
in the stick jail, say I may come
to see your important work
your police book, your boss and your elephant mum
(who really cares and tells you not to play there
because you get dirty
in your stick jail)

I follow you   I'm curious
at last admitted to where you
rid your world of evils

we stop at the carraganas
you enter the thicket
it's a jail you say,
I'm working
you can go away now

tomahawk dream

your shrieks call to me
up here in the second storey
your face beaded with fever sweat
not yet the coloured glass
that will come
a later part of the rite

the tomahawk from the fire sale
real and yours for the killing
it's only a dream I call only a dream
stumbling in the dark towards your room
stroking your head your face   my hand
bumps over the glass whisker beads
as they smoothe and flatten

we had the same dream

I pick the glass out of my hand

You owe me the first phrases

The cello's shoulder held tight to your breastbone
you jostle, startle, then comfort the strings
to make the wind sough, bells ring
then melody a snowy flag: masculine.

From my seat in the audience I am thinking
there are no other people in this concert hall.

No, for me there is only you, and I claim
your legs which cradle the bloom of cello hip
the same legs that taught yourself to ride a tricycle,
getting stronger and stronger as
you ran in your red-fast shoes.
And I watched.

You are the only one, and I claim
your eyes as round in song
as they were at sight of the moon
when you were one and I held you
to see it under the June night sky.
Your brain which I fed with whole grains and fruit,
strings messages to your fingers
tapered and tough. Same fingers that dismantled
the screen door spring in two minutes flat
and I had to find the screws.

You are the only one
and I claim for myself part of your song
the beginning where your bow hand
starts its slow and graceful drag,
close to the bridge, rosin dust
making puffs, and the strings vibrate: poem.

Walking Out

You probably don't remember the first rite of passage:
leaving home in your shirt
in nothing but your T-shirt
running down green August, afraid
I left you behind, when really I was in the back yard
pulling beets from the wet garden.

Your two-year old body barely escaped collision with a car,
swift legs your salvation
I was helpless to prevent anything
as I ran behind
tire squeals split my ears.

After, I tied bells to the doors
to warn me: you're leaving.

Now those bells cheer me
hanging by red cord at the front door
and green at the back. They herald
your brave self
returning home.

Play

She tells me about Pobie Aster
her friend at night,
Pobie's dog Sinchi Paco,
Sinchi's friends Zancu and Cusi.

They all run fast together on the road with bumpy stones
not like the pavement
in front of our daytime house—
stones so smooth she doesn't wear shoes.
It's always safe; it is before cars.

Lately, she tells me, Pobie comes in the daytime too.

matroyshka on valentine's day

six years ago on this day
you were essence wrapped like
swaddling in my mind
on another valentine's you became flesh
and this one you walk beside me
stop and smile as snow
flakes melt on lips
you borrowed from my mother

we are a matroyshka Katie
the ones we have come from
you and me and all that will
come from you and me
and all that shall go on
new hands in new mitts Katie
long after we are held stiff
and still like dolls
in the mother's frozen body

church

. . . and on the third day he rose again, according to the scriptures and ascended into heaven and sits on the right hand of the Father.

she cries out   that's silly
most people are dead when they die
just dead

    it was better when God never died
    she just kept on being   when Her
    boy died we cried for it
    once a year but
    God just kept on being
    no goldenness in church

we used dollies out of clay
you know   like the tea pot
brown as the dirt in the garden and
pretty smelling smoke was all
around the holy, holy ladies

war

she's ten, wearing her middle blue dress,
her reddish hair from the same dye-lot as her father's,
she sits on the front step in the hot sun

she's been looking at pictures
of starving children and weakened mothers
can't understand why I want to fast for peace
says it's dumb
    women should be big and mean
    like boys and it's good sometimes
    for ladies to get dead and have red
    powder all over their bodies
    it shows they're strong and tough
    and mean to hurt people
    red powder is special
    for holy fighters

she says being hungry
and hating guns isn't fun
but when I say it's better than dead
her eyelids cover those green eyes
I see something she says.
It makes her face grow old

and she cries for a different mother
all dead and buried
with an axe and red powder

Believe Me

With your first blood you baptize yourself
you bleed the red blessing: roses, roses, roses.

And I will build an altar on the kitchen table:
waterlily and chokecherry, high bush cranberry, spearmint.

You will enter the wood at the back of the cottage,
sit where the summer you were five
you spoke silently with an owl
(that summer
you were the most animal
you've ever been, soap and shampoo
could not wash away the wildness,
that summer you were most my child
belonged to no other)
that summer will be your guide.

You will go there in your mind and in the wood
as we have arranged, sit
on a cushion of moss and leaves
          wait

and when the rose is in you
you are ordained in the priesthood
of yourself as you approach our altar
to tell me
what you saw and heard, who you are
               the sky is purple, sage is burning

Magdalene

The leaven is constantly threatened
by drafts this January morning.
I worry the bread dough will not rise.
You worry your dough with playdirt
consecrate it charcoal grey.

Supper time, in candlelight, you break your bread in half
as if holy to serve him, your baby fine hair glorious.
Not like the other time when it was a black veil
and he loved you, made the others jealous,
kissing you full on the lips.

Now if he said those words over bread
you wouldn't laugh, losing your place at table.

Every cell in your body remembers
power, you hold your power close
so they can't touch it.

making bread

Marilyn, my aunt's hands were a lot like yours
only hers made bread twenty years ago
in the way you do
fingers puffed from the kneading
her ring a thin gold line

your blouse is like
the cotton dresses she wore
small prints on dark backgrounds
a new one every few years
all cut from the same pattern
she was a pattern set
in her housedress and
maroon sweater that hugged her
abundant bosom on chilly mornings
before the fire was blown to life
in the wood stove
the flour set on the shelf to warm

her pantry a pattern also
flour, lard, sealers of saskatoons
blue bread pan hanging on the door
everything about her was generous
like you

so when Aunt Melanie said in a harsh voice
HANG YOUR COAT AT THE DOOR
I DON'T CARE HOW YOU BEHAVE AT YOUR HOUSE
I did
as my children do for you

his grandmother from Lethbridge

always said she liked to see
a pair of blinds pulled precisely
to the middle of the windows

it made her feel things must be
right in that house

Masika

It's my eye that bothers me
the way it closes when I want it open, droops
as if sliding away from all I see.
Sometimes I think it was a mistake to come here.
And yet, if I had to live it over again
I would do the same thing.

How we lived then you have no idea.
You think lentils are new? You didn't eat lentils every day
and beans and potatoes
all the time. We were poor.
You've never known it.

It's fine to have books by Stalin and Lenin
in your house but you don't know what they did
to my uncle, my cousin. Why I left.
A good job or better husband
would not have kept me.

I clean other people's dirt up, sometimes,
meet people I like and there are always my Hungarian friends.
(They are the craziest!)
I eat meat often and sometimes chocolate.
Except for the eye, I'm happy.

Eugenia

Eugenia squinting   in her garden   fine lines
under a beige babushka   worn
the traditional way   a peak
to keep the sun out
sweating   hoe in hand

she could go to the old folk's home in Qu'Appelle
she says   but she'd miss her garden

black paths between
onions and garlic stepped on with care
Eugenia in the green
a straight rowed garden now
seven children grown and gone
a cataract on her left eye

she shrugs   *they'll fix it in Regina*
in July, she

sits at a framed garden
of cotton print   smooth stitches
large enough for her to see   a quilt
more stubborn than hollyhocks
to cover a great granddaughter
some spring night

when I think it back   she says
it's been hard

rosary

now she labours little Mary
cheeks puff in analgesic breathing
the lie found out
it's pain beyond pain

at seven years she played dollies
in a tidy pretend house where
scoured noxzema jars and green pop bottles
did not catch light or sparkle

at four years she lay in a hospital bed
a bronchial wheeze worked her chest while
comic books were petals around her head

at two years she waddled
too close to the road

I am supposed to be watching
keeping her safe

now she is taken from me in a wheelchair
my baby sister and in her lap a baby
still wrapped in skin and winter clothing
so close to the edge   balancing
she knows when I say good-bye and
the baby will be beautiful
she'll never be so alone again

Knit Once Removed

No, I didn't make this sweater myself.
My mother did, for my sister, who tired of it.
Now it's mine.
She made one for me too
of the same wool but it was too large.
She unravelled it, reknit it
and still it was too large.
That was the problem in
her watery womb and my childhood:
she couldn't understand when I stopped growing,
became an adult, she
expected me to keep on,
to become massive.
I gave the sweater to the Sally Ann,
thankful I hadn't grown into it.
My sister was
what my mother wanted in a sweater.

Red in Houses

for Mary Elizabeth Grace

A three-sided house, fourth wall missing, she shoved scarlet, lilac, salmon and vermillion sweet peas into a maroon vase. Her amber eyes dreamed for her and her new baby, and all the babies after that.

A brand new house made of all new woods she filled with children, then escaped into the garden, ignored the vegetables (which make kids grow even more) to foster gladioli that screamed their orange-red, shouted inside the yard leaning against the fence, exhausted, firmly rooted, planning to go nowhere.

A big old house this time, 4 solid walls filled with exuberantly growing bodies she needed red more than ever. Three foot high finger prints on all the walls and windows. Mouldy apple cores behind the couch. Regularly and to her horror, tiny limp frogs in the back pockets of size 4 jeans when she did the laundry. Into this house she brought red shoes for herself to wear. Red leather romance with heels. No good for running after kids. Ruby shoes.

Another house, newish and white, another time, all her children grown she had her quiet days at last and in one of these grabbed a dowdy african violet turned pale in January, (always not blooming) and put it into a crimson stemmed glass bowl. Left it. Satisfied. She'd told off the sad afternoon. The violet straightened its shoulder leaves, bloomed soon after, kept its purple flowers.

your words

for Liz

lilacs jiggle on their trees
sweep the deep green of wet grass
as roots
          shoot skyward
waving to the sun

your words are lilacs
pushing purple into my eyes
          sailing me to a scented place
where women are laughing

In praise of Julian of Norwich who gave us the word

en   joy   ment
you en joy me   men
and wom/en do this
all the time.   joy
j: cross, bird, blue, hawker
o : double middle of fool
y: vowel-trick with piece of tail, swallowed
meant in all serious/ness, you said
sleep well my love
sleep   curved in my ear   last sounds
before black conscious/ness,
good woman that she is,
takes my soul's hand into a landless region
my hand still smells gloriously of you

well   deep and restful   well water, good, fine
indigo reflecting pure
as legs in-
tertwine, sweet as peas on a vine
great vessels pulsing
that far from the heart
my love mine/my oh my
en joy
men
t.

Buried Deeper & Deeper

Morning coming down from blue
feathers and cotton,
fresh from morning prayer-dreams
her head directed to the east light.

Down the stairs to yellow
kitchen and eggs, she stirs
and boils and scrapes more yellow.
Sleepy child eyelids inching
their way up for school, children
weaning themselves from the floor register
where they warm their bodies from the feet up,
mourning loss of their beds for another day.

She is safer and safer as she sinks
through the morning's light
into the brown rug in the study,
sinks into the basement's accumulation &
collection of thread, silks, cottons.

A soft place to land, padded cell
spiked with bikes and skis, broken
by a teakwood cupboard made by her lover for her cloth.

Some days she's stuck between storeys,
the sinking in her study is stopped
and she is between floors, fir planks
cinching her waist, legs fettered
by white wires strung from joist to joist.

Bones and Black Dresses

She tells us about the treatment
to kill the cancer as she rips lettuce
for a salad. We are in her kitchen
It's five years
since the lumps and the itching.

After dinner she tells us about her swim
from Crete to a dead leper colony on an island,
the walk she took to dry her body,
marble slab she lifted seeing
hundreds of skeletons, headless
all wearing woolly black dresses
and felt shoes with tiny red stitches.

She was stunned, she
walked away from there into
a pleasant cottage where
blinded by sun she nearly
fell into an open cellar among
hundreds of brown skulls.

matins

we dance in the sun, tell all we know
about our dreams from the night before
we wear quilted blue work jackets
babies borne on backs and hips
our black hair shining in china morning light
the babies watch
already know our dreams
but are stilled
by the telling

in June

all of this as I walk to the back of the yard
at eleven thirty   could fall away
the Maltese Cross, Calendula, Wild Bluebell
and Queen Anne's Lace just waking to late spring
sun teasing seeds shy
of the windy songs above

it could all be taken   the sun

could get too hot   could crack my head
along the part in my hair   the seeds
flowers and I never proceeding to noon

Boundary Bay

In this cottage, I respect
the ocean's pull out of my reach
though close enough to hear.
Lost in the sun, I crouch
to see the garden, parched, leeching
salt from the brine.
Vegetables struggle to stand in spite of Grandma
cooking them in the garden from her place in the ether.

Hologram

Since I've been eating vegetables from the sea
I imagine all the cells of my body know:
the slap of aquamarine at their shins,
sharp rocks under their feet,
smells, briny and rotten by turn, lacing
their nostrils and cold that never freezes;
friction and erosion beyond time.

All of which explains my body's less frequent craving
for swimming and salt, water sound and blue.

ACKNOWLEDGEMENTS

I thank the Saskatchewan Arts Board, the Banff Centre, the Ontario Arts Council and the Saskatchewan Writers/Artists Colonies.

I am grateful to the following persons who encouraged and advised during the writing and revising of these poems: Edna Alford, Bonnie Burnard, David Carpenter, Eliza Clark, Don Coles, Lorna Crozier, Lyn King, Elaine Muth, Elizabeth Philips, Steven Smith, Anne Szumigalski, members of the Connaught Group and the Saskatoon Poets Coterie.

I am indebted to my first and present husband, Gordon, for his faith and to my children Katie, Thomas and Patrick for gifts of language and experience.

Some of these poems have been published in: (magazines) *Arc, Antigonish Review, Briarpatch, CVII, Dinosaur Review, event, Fiddlehead, Global Tapestry* (UK), *Grain, New Hope International* (UK), *NeWest Review, Pierian Spring, Prairie Fire, Writing;* (anthologies) *Blue Streak in a Dry Year, Heading Out, Labour Day, Women & Words: The Anthology.* Many of the poems have been broadcast on CBC Radio's "Ambience" and on "Saskatchewan Poets Series" by Brenda Zeman, CKSK-FM Radio, University of Saskatchewan.

SUSAN ANDREWS GRACE

Water is the First World is Susan Andrews Grace's first full collection of poetry. In 1990 Underwhich Editions published a chapbook of her poetry, *Wearing My Father*. Susan's poems have previously appeared in many magazines, including *Ariel*, *A Room of One's Own*, *Arc*, *Antigonish Review*, *Briarpatch*, *Event* and *NeWest Review*, as well as in several anthologies, including Coteau Books' *Heading Out: The New Saskatchewan Poets* (1986).

Susan is also a visual artist who works in textiles. Her quilts and constructions have been part of group and solo exhibitions. In 1986 Susan was the co-designer, maker and co-ordinator of the Peace Quilt for the United Nations International Year of Peace. The Peace Quilt is installed at the Canadian Permanent Mission to the United Nations in New York. As well, Susan is a former nurse, which explains her interest in and strong views on health issues, particularly those that affect women.

Susan was born in Saskatchewan, raised in Manitoba and British Columbia, and currently lives in Saskatoon. In addition to her writing and quilt making she works for CARFAC SASK as an editor and researcher. Susan is an active member of several literary and visual arts organizations.

ABOUT THE COVER ARTIST

Courtney Milne is a Canadian photographer based in Saskatoon. He is well known for his two books on the prairie, *Prairie Light* and *Prairie Dreams*. His latest work, *The Sacred Earth*, is the first of a series of books called The Sacred Earth Collection, a portrayal of the world's most exotic spiritual places. The cover of *Water is the First World* was taken on Oahu, Hawaii, a site sacred to the indigenous Hawaiian people.

MORE POETRY BY WOMEN FROM COTEAU BOOKS

Other poetry from Coteau Books is listed below. You may purchase or order any of these titles from your favorite bookstore. For a complete catalogue of publications—fiction, poetry, drama, criticism, non-fiction and children's literature—please write to Coteau Books at 401-2206 Dewdney Avenue, Regina, Saskatchewan S4R 1H3.

Batoche by Kim Morrissey. A series of poems on the North West Resistance of 1885. Short-listed for the Gerald Lampert Award. ISBN 0-919926-91-6 paper $8.95.

Blue Windows by Catherine M. Buckaway. New and collected poems with lyric elegance from a prolific writer. ISBN 0-919926-89-4 paper $8.00.

Circus Love by Lake Sagaris. The uneasy climate of love, relationships and human rights in Chile, set against the imagery of the circus. ISBN 1-55050-017-1 paper $8.95.

Grasslands by Thelma Poirier. Voices from the grasslands from the time of Sitting Bull to today's ranchers. ISBN 1-55050-006-6 paper $8.95.

Heading Out: The New Saskatchewan Poets edited by Don Kerr and Anne Szumigalski. A sparkling collection of work by Saskatchewan's newer poets. ISBN 0-919926-57-6 paper $9.95.

Maria Breaks Her Silence by Nancy Mattson. A poetic biography of a Finnish immigrant. ISBN 0-919926-92-4 cloth $21.95; ISBN 1-919926-93-2 paper $8.95.

Out of Place: Stories and Poems edited by Ven Begamudré and Judith Krause. An anthology which deals with cultural displacement. ISBN 1-55050-019-8 paper $14.95.

A Sudden Radiance: Saskatchewan Poetry edited by Lorna Crozier and Gary Hyland. A comprehensive collection of work by established poets. ISBN 0-919926-67-3 cloth $21.95; ISBN 0-919926-66-5 paper $14.95.

Time in a Green Country by Elizabeth Philips. "... speaking to us in the language of trees, the language of brome grass, the language of orchids." ISBN 1-55050-005-8 paper $8.95.

White Lions in the Afternoon by Elyse Yates St. George. A book of poetry and visual art. ISBN 0-919926-73-8 cloth $15.00; ISBN 0-919926-72-X paper $7.00.